.75

A Parent's Guide

Home and School
SUCCESS

FIRST GRADE

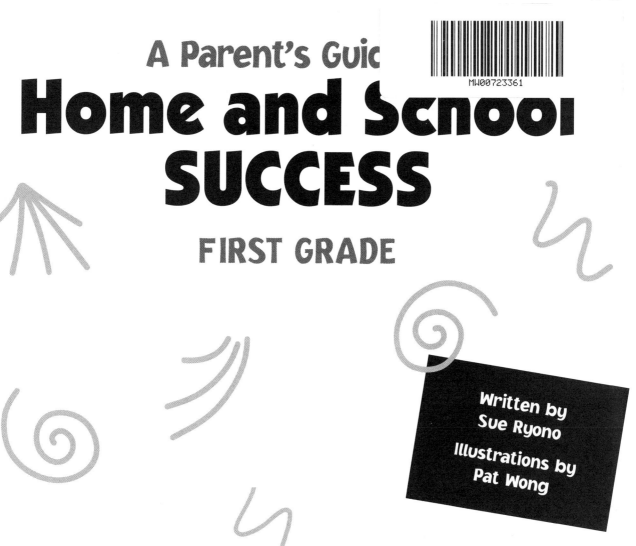

Written by
Sue Ryono

Illustrations by
Pat Wong

MW00723361

Cover Photo © The Stock Market

Photo Credits: © 1997 Comstock, Inc.: 3, 13, 14, 16, 18, 24, 26, 29, 31, 37, 39, 40, 43

Copyright © 1997
This version copyright © 2000 Brighter Vision Publications.
All rights reserved. Except for the inclusion of brief quotations in a review, no part of this book may be reproduced or utilized in any form or by any means, electronic or mechanical, including photocopying, recording, or by any information storage and retrieval system, without written permission from the publisher.

BV15031 Home and School Success: First Grade
Published by Brighter Vision Publications, 225 Duncan Mill Road, Don Mills, Ontario, Canada M3B 3K9
TM is a trademark of Brighter Vision Publications.
Printed in the U.S.A.

Table of Contents

Introduction

Academic Skills

Social Skills

Home and School Cooperation

Rewards

The Fascinating
First Grader!

Parents wear many hats every day. Each one is equally important, but sometimes parents are nervous about wearing the hat of "teacher" for their child. The truth is that all day, every day, the invisible "teacher hat" is perched on your head, perhaps even on top of another hat you may be wearing at the moment! The joy of parenting comes with making the most of every opportunity to be your child's teacher.

Parents can be nervous about performing the role of teacher because they are not sure what expectations or goals are realistic for their child at each level. This book is aimed at helping you understand, appreciate, and accentuate the learning that your child is ready to experience.

You were and still are your child's first and most important teacher. By becoming familiar with the skills a first grader needs, you can be more efficient and effective as you continue in that role.

* They are **sincere**. They express honest opinions without hesitation.

* They are **creative**. Their ability to imagine stories and invent games is unlimited.

* They are **curious** about the world around them and take pleasure in the thrill of discovery.

* They are **generous**. They will share their friendship, thoughts, and feelings with people of all ages.

* They are **marvelous**. They have an immeasurable capacity to learn and love.

* They are **playful**. Join them in a game and share in their laughter.

* They are **sensitive**. Their feelings can be easily hurt and they can recognize the feelings of others.

* They are **exhilarated** when they learn something new.

* They are **eager** to succeed and need plenty of encouragement.

* They are **ready to learn and grow** with your direction and the ideas in this book.

The Keys to Using This Book

Be a Learner

Be ready to tell your child that you don't know something. A question from your child indicates interest in the topic, but you don't need to feel embarrassed if you don't know the answer. The important step is to help him or her look for an answer.

Teach to the Moment

Remember that the best time to teach anything is the moment your child has expressed curiosity about it. If your child asks a question about the phases of the moon, try to provide information, look it up with him or her in a science book or encyclopedia, and watch the sky. If you have access to the Internet or a computer with a multimedia reference tool, use that to gain instant facts to share.

Teach Academic Skills

The first section of this book provides a guide for you that is full of activities that center around the topics first graders study in school. Use it to help your child better understand a topic that is being taught and to enhance what your child is learning at school. Use it as background information to provide ideas for you to use when interacting with your child.

Teach Social Skills

The next section centers around social skills. Even the most intelligent child will be less successful in school without good personal skills. These interpersonal skills are critical for positive relationships to develop and for your child to feel worthwhile. Use this section to provide an approach to a problem or an opening to discuss a topic. With prior discussion about these vital skills, your child will have strategies to deal with concerns when they appear.

Promote Home and School Cooperation

The next section of the book gives you practical ideas for how to navigate home and school interaction on a daily basis. There are suggestions for organizing, communicating with the educational community, conferencing with teachers, and getting involved at school.

Give Praise

Included in the book are reward items. Use these to show your child that you are proud of his or her efforts. Children respond to positive reinforcement. Teachers know that the more specific the praise, the better. "Good job!" is great to hear, but more repeat performances come from phrases such as "You wrote that story so neatly that it is easy for me to read. That shows me you are proud of it, too!"

Learning About READING

Schoolwork is easier and more fun for students who enjoy reading. You can help your child build the necessary skills for becoming a fluent reader and at the same time encourage a love of reading that will last a lifetime.

There are many strategies for teaching reading. You may have heard of phonics instruction, sight-word practice, or a whole-language approach. All of these strategies are helpful in a complete reading program. This book will provide you with a variety of activities to choose from.

PHONICS

Phonics instruction teaches the student the sounds commonly associated with each letter of the alphabet or combinations of letters. Many words can be "sounded out" using a phonics approach. Pages 5–7 describe activities and provide word lists that will help your child learn and practice the letter sounds. Most first graders benefit from a review of the letter sounds. Some first-grade children need to review the alphabet, particularly the lowercase letters. They can then progress to instruction on more complex phonics skills, such as vowels (*a, e, i, o, u*).

SIGHT WORDS

It is helpful for young readers to know the most common words on sight. Words recognized as a whole, without sounding out the individual letters, are called sight words. On page 8, activities are suggested to help your child practice sight-word vocabulary. The English language includes many words that cannot be sounded out using a simple set of phonetic rules so it is important to develop a good sight-word vocabulary.

WORD FAMILIES

Beginning readers enjoy finding patterns and rhyming words. Sometimes groups of words with similar spellings are called word families.

READING ACTIVITIES

A rich variety of reading and writing activities will help your child become a fluent and enthusiastic reader.

The language activities provided on pages 13 through 18 will continue to improve your child's reading skills.

TEACHING READING

Phonics Instruction— teaching the sounds associated with letters or combinations of letters

Sight-Word Method (also called Key-Word Method)—teaching students to recognize whole words, often using flashcards, charts, and basal readers

Whole-Language Instruction—a method of teaching reading that is based primarily on quality literature and the child's own creative writing with less drill on phonics, spelling, and grammar

Literature-based Instruction—similar to the Whole-Language Method, reading is practiced using a rich variety of children's literature instead of a basal reader or phonics instruction

Basal Readers— textbooks that teach reading using stories and activities that start out with a very limited number of words and gradually add more reading vocabulary in succeeding chapters

Controlled-Vocabulary Books—books written using only a very limited number of simple words so that beginning readers can be successful, for example *Hop on Pop* by Dr. Seuss

Sounding Out— the reader combines the individual letter sounds to decode the word

Context Clues—clues such as the meaning of other words in the sentence, the pictures, and the starting letter that enable the reader to figure out an unknown word

Reading Comprehension—the ability to understand the meaning of what one reads

Consonants— the letters *b, c, d, f, g, h, j, k, l, m, n, p, q, r, s, t, v, w, x, y, z*

Vowels—the letters *a, e, i, o, u,* and sometimes *y* (as in *cry* and *baby*)

Short Vowels—the sounds the vowels make in c*a*t, p*e*t, s*i*t, h*o*t, and n*u*t

Long Vowels—the sounds the first vowels make in l*a*ne, m*ea*t, k*i*te, h*o*me, and c*u*te

Blends—two or more consonants sounded together such as *fl* in float or *str* in stripe

Consonant Digraphs— two consonants that combine to make one sound, such as *th*, *ch*, and *sh*

Tips

* Give appealing children's books for birthday and holiday gifts.

* Make library visits a regular habit.

* Help your child obtain a library card of his or her own.

* Select books that appeal to you and your child.

* Remember paperback books are a great value, especially through school book clubs.

* Ham it up when you read aloud—laugh, howl, cry, cackle, and vary your voice.

* Take turns reading with your child—don't turn it into drudgery.

* Set an example by reading books, magazines, newspapers, and recipes yourself!

* Take advantage of handy reading materials, such as contest rules printed on a cereal box.

BEGINNING PHONICS

Scavenger Hunt

Select a consonant and write it on a large piece of paper in both uppercase and lowercase letters. Tell your child the most common sound this letter makes when it begins a word. With your child, search the house and yard to find objects that start with the sound. Look through old magazines, catalogs, and junk mail to find pictures of objects that start with the letter making that sound. Cut them out and paste them to the paper to make a poster. Make a display including the poster and some of the smaller objects you found around the house. Your child may enjoy explaining the display to a friend or to Grandma. This activity can be repeated until you have covered all 21 consonants. Then try the activity featuring short vowels, long vowels, or the digraphs *sh-, ch-,* and *th-.*

I Spy

One player looks around and selects a secret object, such as a bed. This player announces to the rest of the players, "I spy with my little eye something that begins with *b.*" The other players ask questions that can be answered *yes* or *no.* (Examples: Is it alive? Could I eat it? Is it green? Is it smaller than my fist?) Each player takes a turn selecting the object and answering the questions until the object is guessed.

Pack Your Suitcase!

This memory game helps your child review the alphabet as well as the letter sounds. The first player says this verse, filling the blank with anything starting with the letter *a: My Aunt Edna went to Japan, and she took with her some _____.* The next player repeats the verse including the object beginning with *a* and adds another object to the list beginning with *b.* Each player in turn repeats the verse adding an object beginning with the next letter of the alphabet. The game ends when a player cannot recall the list or cannot think of an object to add to the list. Can you make it to *z?* You can personalize the game by using the name of a favorite relative or destination of your own. For example, *My Uncle Tony went to Tucson and he took with him some . . . .*

You can help your child associate sounds with letters using the activities on this page.

Bouncing the Ball

The first player says the following jingle, filling in words that start with the letter *a.*

My name is _____
And my husband's name is ___
And we come from _____
And we sell _____!

The player bounces a ball and passes it under his or her leg when the last word in the last line is spoken. (Of course, boys say *wife* instead of *husband.*) The next player says the same jingle, substituting a word beginning with *b* at the end of each line. Players take turns and try to get all the way to the letter *z.* You may need to look in a dictionary, a book of names, or on a globe to find words beginning with the more unusual letters, such as *Q, X, Y,* and *Z.*

WORD FAMILIES

Once children are familiar with the consonant and short vowel sounds, they are ready to work with simple rhyming words and word families. Help your child sound out these words. The words in each list rhyme with the word pictured at the top.

cat	fan	bed	net	pig
rat	pan	fed	jet	wig
hat	man	red	yet	jig
bat	can	led	get	big
fat	Dan	wed	let	dig
mat	ran	Ted	met	fig
pat	tan	Ned	pet	rig
sat	van	Ed	wet	gig

lip	dog	mop	bug	sun
dip	log	top	tug	bun
hip	fog	hop	hug	fun
nip	bog	pop	rug	run
rip	hog	cop	mug	nun
sip	jog	bop	jug	pun
tip	cog	sop	dug	gun

MORE WORD FAMILIES

These word families include more advanced letter combinations. Teach your child this rhyme: *When two vowels go walking, the first one does the talking!* It indicates that when two vowels are close together, the first vowel becomes a long vowel and the second vowel is silent. The words in each list rhyme with the word pictured at the top of the column. Have your child read each list.

  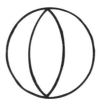  

pail	hay	ball	jeep	nine
sail	bay	call	beep	mine
tail	day	fall	keep	dine
hail	lay	hall	deep	fine
jail	may	mall	peep	line
mail	pay	tall	weep	vine
nail	say	wall	sheep	wine
rail	play	small	sleep	shine

light	king	nose	blue	cry
night	ring	hose	due	by
might	sing	rose	Sue	my
right	wing	pose	clue	fly
sight	thing	close	glue	try
fight	sting	those	true	why

SIGHT WORDS

Make flashcards to help your child develop his or her sight-word vocabulary. Start out with just three words from this list. Print each word on two separate index cards. Practice with this mini-deck of six cards the first day. Each day add a new word on two more cards to the deck. In a few months, your child will recognize almost one hundred words on sight!

> Fluent readers do not sound out each word. They recognize common words on sight. Here are some very common words that should become part of your child's sight-word vocabulary.

a	by	did	had	into	me	on	some	two	where
an	but	down	her	just	more	old	so	up	when
and	been	each	here	know	my	one	the	very	why
at	big	for	has	like	much	or	that	was	will
am	can	first	have	little	no	our	there	we	with
as	call	from	how	love	not	other	they	want	write
all	came	get	I	look	new	out	them	went	yes
are	come	go	in	made	now	said	their	were	you
about	do	he	is	make	of	see	this	who	your
be	dear	him	it	many	off	she	to	what	

Activities with sight-word flashcards:

✳ Read the words to your child.

✳ Have your child make pairs of the cards with matching words.

✳ Have your child read the words to you.

✳ If your child prefers action, spread the cards on the floor face up. One player calls out a word. The other player must stand with each foot on a card with that word. Your child will enjoy being the caller and making you hop around, too. It's still great reading practice!

What if your child finds a particular word hard to remember?

✳ You can tape copies of this word on the front door, on your forehead, or inside a lunchbox if you think your child will find these reminders funny.

✳ Have your child type words on a typewriter or computer to make his or her own reminders.

✳ Have your child spell out the word with alphabet cereal and eat it.

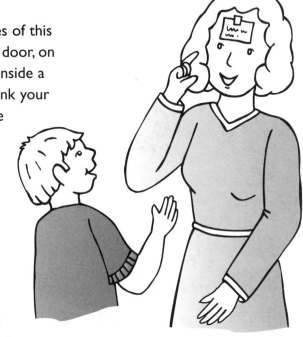

HURRAY FOR BEDTIME STORIES!

Children can appreciate literature and information that is much too difficult for them to read independently, so adults must continue to read exciting, challenging books to beginning readers. One of the best things parents and teachers can do for children of any age is to read aloud to them. Building enthusiasm for books and learning is just as important as developing the mechanical skills of reading!

Young children do need to have simplified reading materials available so that they can successfully practice reading independently. However, if all of the books they see are textbooks about a "fat cat that sat on a hat" or "Dick and Jane and their dog Spot," children may come to think of reading as a boring, mechanical skill.

The following annotated list will help you find some of the perennial read-aloud favorites, but you will want to select books that are especially appealing to your own tastes and interests. Children's books may be sweet and sentimental or wickedly humorous. The artwork may be comical cartoons, gorgeous full-colored paintings, or whimsical folk art. Each family will find particular authors and illustrators they especially enjoy.

PICTURE BOOKS

Author/Illustrator: Tomie de Paola—This author's whimsical folk art complements his retelling of traditional stories.
The Legend of the Bluebonnet (Putnam, 1983)
Fin M'Coul (Holiday, 1981)

Author: Arthur Dorros—
Dorros writes appealing fiction and nonfiction works, many of which are available in a Spanish version.
Abuela

This Is My House
Written and illustrated by Arthur Dorros

(Dutton, 1991)
This Is My House (Scholastic, 1992)

Author/Illustrator: P. D. Eastman—After you read aloud these fun, friendly books, your child may want to try reading them to you.
Are You My Mother? (Random House, 1960)
Go, Dog, Go (Random House, 1961)

Author/Illustrator: Lois Ehlert—Bold art, large text, and small captions mix to make Ehlert's books great for a variety of readers.
Growing Vegetable Soup

(Harcourt Brace, 1987)
Snowballs (Harcourt Brace, 1995)

Author/Illustrator: Ezra Jack Keats—Keats's beautiful collage artwork enhances stories featuring African-American characters.
Whistle for Willie (Viking, 1964)
John Henry (Pantheon, 1965)

Author/Illustrator: Steven Kellogg—Children love the sunny, humorous artwork in Kellogg's many fine children's books.
The Mysterious Tadpole (Dial, 1977)
The Island of the Skog (Dial, 1973)

PICTURE BOOKS

Author/Illustrator:
Bill Peet—Peet's humorous stories teach important lessons about kindness, being yourself, and conservation.
The Whingdingdilly (Houghton Mifflin, 1970)
The Wump World (Houghton Mifflin, 1970)

Author/Illustrator:
Patricia Polacco—Polacco's expressive illustrations and tender stories appeal to children and adults.
Thunder Cake (Philomel, 1990)
Mrs. Katz and Tush (Bantam, 1992)

Author/Illustrator: Faith Ringgold—Ringgold's stylish books tell of hopes and dreams within the African-American community and beyond.
Tar Beach (Crown, 1991)
My Dream of Martin Luther King (Crown, 1995)

Author/Illustrator:
Dr. Seuss—His humorous rhyming stories often teach an important social lesson about honesty, self-worth, or environmental responsibility.
The Lorax (Random House, 1971)
Green Eggs and Ham (Random House, 1960)

Author: Judith Viorst—Viorst writes unsentimental, often humorous stories about contemporary children and their daily problems.
The Tenth Good Thing About Barney (Macmillan, 1971)
Alexander and the Terrible, Horrible, No Good, Very Bad Day (Macmillan, 1972)

SERIES

Author/Illustrator: Marc Brown
Publisher: Little, Brown and Company
Arthur's Teacher Trouble

Author: Russell Hoban
Publisher: HarperCollins
Bedtime for Frances

Author/Illustrator: Arnold Lobel
Publisher: HarperCollins
Frog and Toad Together

Author: Else Holmelund Minarik
Publisher: HarperCollins
Little Bear

Author: Cynthia Rylant
Publisher: Bradbury
Henry and Mudge: The First Book

Each of these authors has a series of books about a lovable animal character. One title from the series is listed to get you started.

Author/Illustrator:
Bernard Waber
Publisher: Houghton Mifflin
Lyle, Lyle, Crocodile

FOLK TALES AND FAIRY TALES

These stories are part of our country's diverse cultural heritage. The versions listed here are single-story picture books. You may also want to look for collections of Greek myths; stories by Hans Christian Andersen, the Brothers Grimm, or Charles Perrault; Uncle Remus stories from the South; and Native American tales from your region or beyond.

Aardema, Verna. *Who's In Rabbit's House?* (Dial, 1977)

Brett, Jan. *The Mitten* (Putnam, 1989)

Bruchac, Joseph. *The Great Ball Game* (Dial, 1994)

Climo, Shirley. *The Korean Cinderella* (HarperCollins, 1993)

Ehrlich, Amy. *The Wild Swans* (Dial, 1981)

Grimm, Brothers. *The Twelve Dancing Princesses* illustrated by Errol Le Cain (Viking, 1978)

Kimmel, Eric. *Anansi and the Moss-Covered Rock* (Holiday, 1988)

Kipling, Rudyard. *The Elephant's Child* illustrated by Lorinda Bryan Cauley (Harcourt Brace, 1983)

McDermott, Gerald. *Coyote* (Harcourt Brace, 1994)

Xiong, Blia. *Nine-in-One! Grr! Grr!* (Children's Book Press, 1989)

CHILDREN'S NOVELS

Author: Beverly Cleary—Cleary writes entertaining stories about everyday children. She has a popular series of books featuring a spunky girl named Ramona.

Ramona the Pest (Morrow, 1968)

Author: E. B. White—Children who are ready to listen to longer books with chapters will enjoy these classics.

Charlotte's Web (HarperCollins, 1952)

Stuart Little (HarperCollins, 1945)

POETRY

Make sure to include poetry in your read aloud repertoire. The few minutes it takes to read a poem may brighten up your family for hours!

Falling Up by Shel Silverstein (HarperCollins, 1996) [Look for his best-selling earlier volumes as well—*Where the Sidewalk Ends* and *A Light in the Attic*.]

Honey, I Love by Eloise Greenfield (Crowell, 1978)

The Random House Book of Poetry for Children selected by Jack Prelutsky (Random House, 1983)

FIRST READING BOOKS

Most children need to practice with controlled-vocabulary books when they are first learning to read. These books use a small number of words with motivating pictures to help emerging readers have successful reading experiences. Ask at the public library about books for the beginning reader. Inexpensive paperback series of easy reading books are available at school supply stores, bookstores, and some toy stores. You can also make controlled-vocabulary books for your child. Here's how:

Book One

Use photographs, pictures clipped from catalogs, junk mail, or magazines, or make your own drawings of easily recognizable objects. In this first book, your child will be practicing the words *I, see, a,* and *an*. Under each picture, print a descriptive sentence such as "I see a bunny." Each sentence begins with "I see a . . ." Your child can guess the last word in each sentence from looking at the picture. Staple the pages together and add a cover. You may want to pick a theme for this book, such as animals or vehicles, depending on your supply of pictures.

Book Two

Construct this book as you did Book One, except the words taught in this book are *see* and *the*. Under each picture, write a sentence such as "See the tractor." Again, your child will guess the last word from the picture.

Book Three

In this book, your child will practice reading the words *this, is,* and *my* as well as reviewing words learned in Book One and Book Two. Place interesting pictures on each page. Family photographs come in handy. You can use up the goofy ones you chose not to put in the family album. Under each picture, write a simple descriptive sentence, such as these: *This is my mom. This is a horse. This is the fire station.* Again, the last word in each sentence can be inferred from the picture.

Review

Make flashcards of the words learned in the first three beginning books: *I, see, a, an, the, this, is,* and *my*. You may have already made flashcards for these words from the common sight-word list on page 8. Make two copies of each word. Your child can practice reading these words and play *Scramble* and *Concentration* with them as well (see page 23).

More Books

You can make additional reading books using the following sentence patterns:

Can you see the dog?
Yes, I see the dog.
(New words: *can, you, yes*)

Is this a cat?
No, it is not. (or Yes, it is a cat.)
(New words: *no, not, it*)

I see one cat.
I see two apples.
(New words: number words *one* to *ten*)

I see a red shirt.
I see a blue ball.
(New words: color words)

Learning About Language Arts

In first grade, students will be learning to express themselves in writing. Sample alphabets are printed on page 15. Check with your child's school to find out which manuscript (printing) style is being taught. Remember, your child will be expected to write using both the uppercase and lowercase letters.

The most basic spelling, grammar, and punctuation skills are introduced in first grade, but students are not expected to write without errors at this age! Encourage your child to write out stories, letters, greeting cards, reminders, invitations, valentines, journal entries, apologies, lists, contracts, and signs. Don't always be particular about correct spelling and form. Aunt Jennifer will treasure the letter little Danny sends her even if it does ask her how she likes being a "fizzicks" professor. When your child is ready, you can introduce and practice some of the grammar and punctuation concepts presented on the pages that follow.

Children continue to develop their speaking ability throughout their years in school. The suggested activities on page 18 will give your child an opportunity to improve his or her oral language skills. Developing a wide speaking vocabulary and learning to communicate effectively will contribute to success in school and in life.

Writing stories and poetry will be part of first-grade language assignments. But you can incorporate writing into ordinary family activities. For example, your child can write thank-you notes for birthday and holiday gifts. Grandparents, aunts, uncles, and teachers will appreciate handmade greeting cards. School friends who are ill will appreciate a get-well card and a summary of interesting school events happening during their absence. As you plan a special birthday party, your child can write out lists of supplies, games, and guests. Some children even enjoy making their own invitations, either hand-written or on the computer.

Family life can be quite hectic with jobs, school, homework, day care, extracurricular activities, and longer commutes. You may find days passing without a chance to have a relaxed conversation with your child. You may have to make a point to schedule time to communicate! Some parents use dinnertime or bedtime as a

special time to chat about the day's events. Others use the family car as a conference room as they commute to activities. Resourceful working parents may want to use their break time for a telephone chat.

You don't have to be physically present to exchange ideas with your child. Write a letter! Remember to print and keep the reading level simple. Add a little cartoon to illustrate the words—even if all you can draw is stick figures, your child will love it. A loving note or reminder can be tucked in your child's lunchbox or backpack. For children who are not yet reading, leave a recorded message on the answering machine or tape recorder. If you ask questions in your communication, your child will be encouraged to write or tape a reply.

TEACHING LANGUAGE ARTS

Language Arts—the four main communication areas of reading, writing, speaking, and listening

Manuscript Printing—the style of printing used to write in the primary grades (see page 15)

Cursive Writing—connected handwriting, usually taught in third grade

Punctuation—the use of marks in writing to clarify meaning; first-grade instruction usually focuses on the period, question mark, and exclamation point, and apostrophes used in contractions

Capitalization—the use of an uppercase letter to begin a sentence or a proper noun; first graders are also taught to capitalize the pronoun *I*

Parts of Speech—[noun, verb, adjective, and so on] first graders are introduced to the concept of naming words (nouns), action words (verbs), and describing words (adjectives), but are usually not expected to identify the parts of speech

Prewriting—gathering ideas and organizing information before writing a draft

Writing Prompt—a suggested topic, story starter, experience, or instruction that gives the student something to write about

Invented Spelling—(also called phonetic spelling) the attempted spelling of a word by children based on the sounds, letter combinations, and spelling patterns they know (Example: *rite* instead of *write*); gradually children learn how to spell the word from receiving guidance in correcting their written work, seeing it repeatedly in their reading, or by formally studying the correct spelling

Conventional Spelling—the word as spelled in the dictionary; the correct spelling

Tips

✳ Pencils with a fairly soft lead (No. 2) require less pressure.

✳ Nontoxic, colorful felt-tip pens inspire many children to make signs and greeting cards.

✳ Some young children do not have the fine-motor coordination to write neatly in first grade no matter how hard they try. They may prefer to dictate longer stories to an adult.

✳ With adult supervision, your child will enjoy typing messages on a computer or typewriter.

MANUSCRIPT ALPHABET

Aa Bb Cc Dd Ee Ff

Gg Hh Ii Jj Kk Ll

Mm Nn Oo Pp Qq Rr

Ss Tt Uu Vv Ww Xx

Yy Zz

MODERN MANUSCRIPT ALPHABET

Aa Bb Cc Dd Ee Ff

Gg Hh Ii Jj Kk Ll

Mm Nn Oo Pp Qq Rr

Ss Tt Uu Vv Ww Xx

Yy Zz

WRITING PROJECTS

Most first-grade students can think a hundred times faster than they can write. You may want to start out taking dictation as your child narrates a story or composes a letter. Be sure to use correct manuscript printing with both uppercase and lowercase letters. If you keep the text short enough, your child may enjoy typing the composition on a computer or typewriter or rewriting it in his or her own printing. Some children benefit from tracing over the light pencil letters written by a parent. A felt-tip pen with a fine point is handy for tracing.

Imagine what fun you could have with a giant butterfly . . .

Greeting Cards

Holidays, birthdays, the illness of a friend or relative, and graduations are just a few of the occasions that call for sending a card. You'll save money, add a personal touch, and reinforce writing skills if you have your child write and illustrate the cards. Have friends and relatives save greeting cards for you to use as samples or use the pictures to embellish your child's creations. Save greeting card catalogs for more ideas. For an exciting challenge, try making pop-up cards using the ideas in Joan Irvine's *How to Make Pop-Ups* (Morrow Jr. Books, 1988).

Journals

Many writers keep a daily journal. You can help your child establish a writing habit by starting a daily journal. Each day your child can write or dictate thoughts, feelings, or anecdotes about the day's events. You may have to prompt your child with tactful questions at first, such as "Do you want to write about that big spider you found in the bathtub?" or "Tell me about recess on the big playground."

Super Pets

Not every child can own a real, live pet. But everyone can have fun thinking of the ideal imaginary pet. Read *Clifford, the Big Red Dog* by Norman Bridwell (Scholastic, 1963) to your child and talk about what it would be like to have a huge dog like Clifford. Then let your child invent a special pet and write about their adventures together. Imagine what fun you could have with a giant butterfly, a tame dolphin, a talking eagle, or a friendly dinosaur! Read Syd Hoff's *Danny and the Dinosaur* (HarperCollins, 1958) for further inspiration.

SPELLING ACTIVITIES

Children are motivated to learn how to spell words that have special meaning for them. Every child should learn how to spell his or her first and last names. The common words listed under sight-word vocabulary (page 8) are also appropriate for your child to learn to spell because they come up so frequently in reading and writing. Word families, as shown on pages 6 and 7, are also satisfying to learn to spell because one pattern can be applied to spelling many words.

Once your child begins the writing activities, you might want to make a chart labeled "My Words" for your child. When your child asks you how to spell a word, consider adding it to this list. Later, you can refer your child to this chart to locate how to spell frequently used words.

You can also put together a mini-dictionary for your child. Staple together 26 sheets of paper. Decorate the cover and write a letter of the alphabet in the upper, right-hand corner of each page. When your child asks you how to spell frequently used words, print the word neatly under the correct letter of the alphabet. This book can then be used for reference in future writing assignments.

Don't expect your child to sound out all of the words in the English language and spell them correctly without spelling practice. Notice that many common words, such as *was, been, could, of, said, because,* and *come,* do not follow regular phonics rules. These and other words may require special practice.

Here are some activities you can do to practice spelling words from school lists or ones you compose together at home.

Word Detective—For very common words, have your child go through old ads and magazine articles highlighting the spelling word every time it appears in the text.

Word Puzzles—Write the spelling word in bold letters on cardboard. Cut the letters apart with curved cuts to make a puzzle. Have your child put the word back together.

This bug is red.

Scrambled Words—Write a list of your child's spelling words with the letters in mixed-up order for your child to unscramble.

Word Hunt—Print spelling words on a sheet of large-box graph paper, one letter per square. Fill in the blank spaces with random letters. Your child must find and circle the hidden spelling words.

Cartoon Time—Children who love to draw can make a cartoon illustration for each spelling word. Under the cartoon, the spelling word is underlined in a sentence describing the picture. For funny examples, read *The Cat in the Hat Beginner Book Dictionary* by P. D. Eastman (Random House, 1964).

ORAL LANGUAGE

Although your child is starting to practice written language skills, it is very important to develop oral language skills, too. Here are some activities to expand your child's vocabulary and oral language skills.

Dress-Up Corner

Use make-believe situations to get your child to talk up a storm. Collect hats, shoes, dresses, ties, dishes, dolls, and other materials your child can use to play house. A toy medical kit and some stuffed animals can set the stage for playing veterinarian. Canned goods, boxes, grocery sacks, fruits, and vegetables from your kitchen can be used to set up a pretend grocery store. If you use real money, this will also reinforce math skills. Your child will enjoy putting a price on each item, totaling up the bill on a hand calculator, and counting up the day's receipts.

Field Trips

You and your child will have more to talk about if you go on mini-field trips. Trips to the zoo and the seashore are great for special occasions, but you can also observe the insects living in your garden or the animals at a nearby pet store. Call the local fire station (the public information number, not the emergency number) to find out when it has an open house. Your child will also enjoy visiting a parent's workplace.

Hurray for Grandparents

Doting relatives who live far away miss talking to your child. Tape an interview with your child to send to a relative. Your child might want to read a poem, sing a song, or add other dramatic personal touches to the tape. If it's not too expensive, let your child have a turn talking on the telephone to special relatives. Talking on the telephone encourages the child to speak up in a clear tone of voice.

On With the Show

Many children enjoy putting on a play, circus, or puppet show. Your collection of dress-up clothes will come in handy. Making tickets, popping popcorn, and setting up a lemonade stand will add a realistic touch. As the children plan and narrate the show, they are developing valuable communication skills. You don't need a fancy stage or professional costumes, just use materials at hand and a generous dose of imagination. Dolls and stuffed animals can be used in place of puppets, or children can make their own puppets. They can hide behind the couch to simulate a puppet stage. Children may enjoy acting out well-known nursery rhymes and fairy tales, fables, or religious stories they have studied.

Learning About Math

First-grade students are learning how to add and subtract; write numbers; read number words to 100; use math symbols; identify geometric shapes; measure; construct graphs; identify patterns; solve simple word problems; use math vocabulary; handle money; count by ones, twos, fives, and tens to 100; estimate sensible answers; think logically; and measure time by hours, days, weeks, months, and seasons. Worksheets and flashcards can be helpful, but there are all kinds of practical, interesting activities around your home and neighborhood that will reinforce these concepts as well.

Hang an attractive calendar at eye level for your child to keep track of appointments, birthdays, holidays, and special events. This will help you stay organized as your child practices important calendar skills.

When setting the table, your child can take satisfaction in being helpful and in practicing counting skills and problem solving skills as well.

Mixing up the pancake batter for a special weekend breakfast will give your child practice in reading recipes, measuring volume, and using fractions!

Giving your child an easy-to-use personal alarm clock will not only encourage punctuality, it also helps teach telling time.

As your child saves up change to pay for that special toy, you will have a natural opportunity to teach the value of each coin.

If you cut six oranges into quarters for the three kids playing in the yard, they can have an interesting math discussion as they try to divide the treats among themselves equally.

Limiting each child to a five-minute turn on the swing helps prevent fights and encourages the children to study a wristwatch very carefully!

Math is all around us! Be alert to the opportunities in your family's daily routines.

TEACHING MATH

Place Value—the change in the value of a digit due to its position in a number; Example: 592—the 5 represents 5 *hundreds*, the 9 represents 9 *tens*, and the 2 represents 2 *ones*

Ordinals—number words that show order, such as *first, second, third*, and so on

Set—a collection of objects or numbers that can be counted

Manipulatives—real objects such as buttons or blocks used to illustrate concepts or to solve problems

Computation—finding the correct answer using addition, subtraction, multiplication, or division

Sum—the answer in an addition problem

Difference—the answer in a subtraction problem

Numerator—the number above the line in a fraction that tells how many parts there are

Denominator—the number below the line in a fraction that tells how many equal parts make a whole

$$\frac{3}{4} \quad \begin{array}{l}\leftarrow \text{numerator} \\ \leftarrow \text{denominator}\end{array}$$

Metric System—the system of measurement used by most countries; its basic units include the meter, liter, and gram

U.S. Customary System—the system of measurement used by the United States; its basic units include inches, feet, miles, cups, quarts, ounces, and pounds

Geometry—the branch of mathematics that deals with points, lines, and shapes

Tips

✳ Shopping trips provide opportunities for math practice as you compare prices, weigh produce, count out change, and estimate totals. Allow twice as much time for your shopping expedition when you include your child—you will both be in a better mood if you are not rushed.

✳ At a fast-food restaurant, give your child money to pay for his or her own meal.

✳ Point out or hunt for geometric shapes—the sandwich cut into triangles or rectangles, the birthday hats that are cones, the can shelf full of cylinders, the ball that is a sphere.

✳ Almost every board game, card game, domino game, or activity with dice teaches a math skill that first graders need to practice. Set aside a family game night each week.

✳ Your child will enjoy checking math answers using a calculator.

✳ Young sports fans will develop their math skills as they study the statistics for their favorite team or players. Study baseball cards and the sports section of the newspaper together.

MATH MANIPULATIVES

If you look around your home, you can find objects to use to illustrate math lessons. Your neighbors and relatives may be able to contribute items to your collection. For example, when your child is working on learning to tell time, practicing setting the time on a collection of old clocks will make it more interesting. Clocks don't have to be in running order to use for this activity.

Buttons, beans, toothpicks, blocks, small toys, beads that snap together or can be 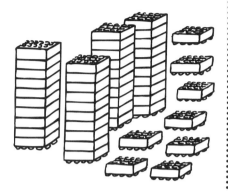 strung on a cord, or even paper clips make handy manipulatives your child can count out, sort by attributes, divide into sets and fractions of sets, or use to illustrate place value. For example, let's say you have a large collection of blocks that snap together and come in many colors. You could illustrate place value by choosing a certain size block to represent ones, and snapping together a column of ten of them to represent tens.

48 = 4 tens and 8 ones

If you don't have blocks, you could illustrate the same concept by bundling ten toothpicks together with a rubber band to represent tens while leaving single,

loose toothpicks to represent the ones.

When your child is learning fractions, you can illustrate the concept of equal parts by cutting an actual pie or pizza into halves, thirds, fourths, or eighths! Dividing a batch of cookies among four children demonstrates fractional parts of a set.

Counting up real money to buy holiday gifts and making real change when playing grocery store will teach the value of money far better than the pictures on a worksheet.

Determining the value of a pile of nickels from the piggybank is a fun way to teach counting by fives. And calculating how many more months until the next birthday will get your child to study the seasons, months, weeks, and days on an actual calendar. Real-life problems are naturally motivating!

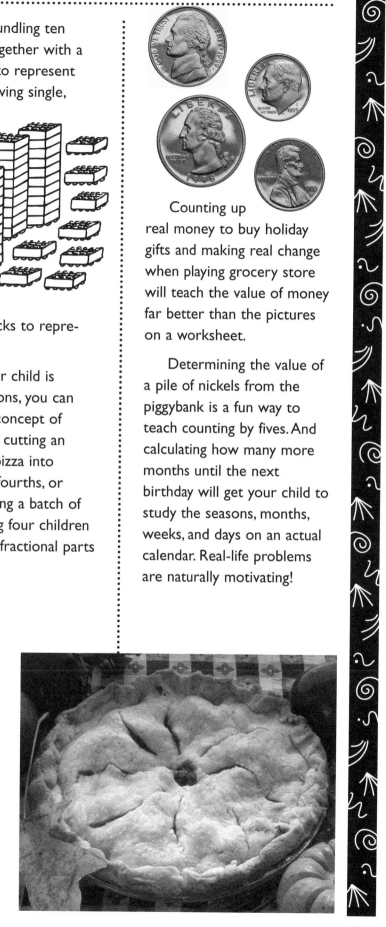

COMPUTATION SKILLS

Be sure to use the horizontal as well as the vertical format when writing problems for practice.

2
+ 2

2 + 2 = ____

vertical format

horizontal or equation format

Addition and subtraction are a major focus of first grade math. All first-grade students should learn the addition and subtraction combinations to 10 shown below.

Addition Facts

0 + 0 = 0	2 + 2 = 4	5 + 0 = 5
0 + 1 = 1	2 + 3 = 5	5 + 1 = 6
0 + 2 = 2	2 + 4 = 6	5 + 2 = 7
0 + 3 = 3	2 + 5 = 7	5 + 3 = 8
0 + 4 = 4	2 + 6 = 8	5 + 4 = 9
0 + 5 = 5	2 + 7 = 9	5 + 5 = 10
0 + 6 = 6	2 + 8 = 10	6 + 0 = 6
0 + 7 = 7	3 + 0 = 3	6 + 1 = 7
0 + 8 = 8	3 + 1 = 4	6 + 2 = 8
0 + 9 = 9	3 + 2 = 5	6 + 3 = 9
1 + 0 = 1	3 + 3 = 6	6 + 4 = 10
1 + 1 = 2	3 + 4 = 7	7 + 0 = 7
1 + 2 = 3	3 + 5 = 8	7 + 1 = 8
1 + 3 = 4	3 + 6 = 9	7 + 2 = 9
1 + 4 = 5	3 + 7 = 10	7 + 3 = 10
1 + 5 = 6	4 + 0 = 4	8 + 0 = 8
1 + 6 = 7	4 + 1 = 5	8 + 1 = 9
1 + 7 = 8	4 + 2 = 6	8 + 2 = 10
1 + 8 = 9	4 + 3 = 7	9 + 0 = 9
1 + 9 = 10	4 + 4 = 8	9 + 1 = 10
2 + 0 = 2	4 + 5 = 9	
2 + 1 = 3	4 + 6 = 10	

Subtraction Facts

0 – 0 = 0	6 – 1 = 5	8 – 8 = 0
1 – 0 = 1	6 – 2 = 4	9 – 0 = 9
1 – 1 = 0	6 – 3 = 3	9 – 1 = 8
2 – 0 = 2	6 – 4 = 2	9 – 2 = 7
2 – 1 = 1	6 – 5 = 1	9 – 3 = 6
2 – 2 = 0	6 – 6 = 0	9 – 4 = 5
3 – 0 = 3	7 – 0 = 7	9 – 5 = 4
3 – 1 = 2	7 – 1 = 6	9 – 6 = 3
3 – 2 = 1	7 – 2 = 5	9 – 7 = 2
3 – 3 = 0	7 – 3 = 4	9 – 8 = 1
4 – 0 = 4	7 – 4 = 3	9 – 9 = 0
4 – 1 = 3	7 – 5 = 2	10 – 1 = 9
4 – 2 = 2	7 – 6 = 1	10 – 2 = 8
4 – 3 = 1	7 – 7 = 0	10 – 3 = 7
4 – 4 = 0	8 – 0 = 8	10 – 4 = 6
5 – 0 = 5	8 – 1 = 7	10 – 5 = 5
5 – 1 = 4	8 – 2 = 6	10 – 6 = 4
5 – 2 = 3	8 – 3 = 5	10 – 7 = 3
5 – 3 = 2	8 – 4 = 4	10 – 8 = 2
5 – 4 = 1	8 – 5 = 3	10 – 9 = 1
5 – 5 = 0	8 – 6 = 2	
6 – 0 = 6	8 – 7 = 1	

Many first graders are ready to learn the addition combinations to 18. Practice these math facts by playing the card games described on the next page. Addition and subtraction of two-digit numbers may also be introduced. First-grade problems usually do not involve regrouping (carrying or borrowing).

2 + 9 = 11	5 + 9 = 14	7 + 7 = 14	8 + 9 = 17
3 + 8 = 11	6 + 5 = 11	7 + 8 = 15	9 + 2 = 11
3 + 9 = 12	6 + 6 = 12	7 + 9 = 16	9 + 3 = 12
4 + 7 = 11	6 + 7 = 13	8 + 3 = 11	9 + 4 = 13
4 + 8 = 12	6 + 8 = 14	8 + 4 = 12	9 + 5 = 14
4 + 9 = 13	6 + 9 = 15	8 + 5 = 13	9 + 6 = 15
5 + 6 = 11	7 + 4 = 11	8 + 6 = 14	9 + 7 = 16
5 + 7 = 12	7 + 5 = 12	8 + 7 = 15	9 + 8 = 17
5 + 8 = 13	7 + 6 = 13	8 + 8 = 16	9 + 9 = 18

CARD GAMES

Playing games with an ordinary deck of cards is a fun way to practice math concepts! The games are listed below in order of concept difficulty, with *Add Them Up* being the most challenging. You may want to further simplify the games by removing the face cards from the deck.

Scramble

Spread out all of the cards faceup. At the word "go," all players try to collect as many pairs as possible. This game teaches number recognition. **Addition Variation:** Choose a target sum, such as 7. Players try to collect as many pairs as possible that add up to 7.

Concentration

Spread out all of the cards in rows facedown. The first player turns over any two cards hoping to find a pair. If the cards match, the player keeps them and takes another turn. If the cards do not match, the player replaces them both facedown, and it is the next player's turn. After all of the cards have been matched, the player with the most pairs wins. This game also reinforces number recognition. **Doubles Variation:** Addition problems where the same two numbers are added, such as 4 + 4, are called "doubles." Require the player to add the doubles in order to keep the matched pair.

War

Players begin with an equal amount of cards stacked facedown. Each player flips over the top card so both players can see it. The card with the greater value captures the pair. If the cards are equal, each player places three cards facedown and a fourth card faceup. The faceup card with the greater value wins all 10 cards! If the cards are equal again, put three facedown and a fourth card faceup until one player wins the entire stack. Captured cards are placed at the bottom of the player's deck. Play continues until one player wins all of the cards. Or if time runs out, the player with the most cards wins. This game reinforces the concepts of "greater than" and "less than."

Add Them Up

Players begin with an equal amount of cards stacked facedown. Each player flips over the top card so both players can see it. The first player to correctly add the numbers together gets to keep them. The captured cards are added facedown to the bottom of the player's deck. Continue playing until a player has won all the cards. To make the game more fair and fun, set a headstart time where the advanced player has to count to five before he or she can call out the answer. **Subtraction Variation:** Instead of adding the two numbers, players subtract to find the difference.

Learning About Science

In first grade, children continue to learn about the needs of living things (both plants and animals), weather, some basic states of matter (solid, liquid, gas), a little kitchen chemistry, the five senses, good health habits, and the scientific method. They make predictions, test their hypotheses, record data, and state their results. Some classes will study the solar system and memorize the names of the planets. Other classes will investigate magnetism and buoyancy. If possible, find out the topics stressed in your child's school and class. Some teachers have an area of special expertise, such as marine biology, that they can share with their students.

Since most first-grade children are just beginning to learn to read, science activities should be based on discussions, explorations, field trips, and hands-on activities. Information in the encyclopedia or most textbooks will be too difficult for the children to read by themselves, but they will appreciate studying the pictures as adults interpret the text for them.

Science activities will give your child an opportunity to review measurement skills such as measuring time, weight, length, and volume. Graphing skills can be practiced as your child charts the growth of a sunflower, puppy, or baby brother. Writing skills improve when keeping a journal for a science fair project. And, of course, science books can reinforce important comprehension skills.

You will not need expensive equipment or a laboratory to explore science with your first-grade child. The people, plants, animals, common objects, and weather in your neighborhood, as well as cooking projects in your kitchen, will provide you with ample material for your little scientist to study.

Every neighborhood is different. Field trips to the tidepools, botanical gardens, zoo, museums, oil refinery, farm, landfill, weather station, bakery, or local power plant may be available. If the school budget is tight, classes may not be able to venture out as a group. However, you can invite another parent and child to join you on interesting expeditions.

SCIENCE

Scientific Method—a method of investigation that involves these steps: stating a hypothesis or guess, designing an experiment, collecting data, and analyzing the results

States of Matter—the three forms matter usually exists in—*solid* (such as ice), *liquid* (such as water), or *gas* (such as steam)

Buoyancy—the tendency to float in air or water

Solar System—the sun and the objects that revolve around it, such as planets and their moons, asteroids, meteors, and comets

Five Senses—taste, smell, touch, sight, and hearing

Habitat—the natural environment in which something lives

Metamorphosis—the distinct changes of form undergone by some animals as they grow, such as a tadpole changing into a frog or a caterpillar changing to a butterfly

Warm-blooded—having blood that stays at about the same temperature even when the temperature of the surrounding air or water changes

Cold-blooded— having blood that changes in temperature when the temperature of the surrounding air or water changes

Mammals—a group of animals that have a backbone, are warm-blooded, usually have hair or fur, and feed their babies milk

Amphibians— a group of animals that have a backbone, are cold-blooded, have moist scaleless skin, and commonly live in water and on land

Reptiles—a group of animals that have a backbone, are cold-blooded, and are covered with scales or horny plates

Birds—a group of animals that have a backbone, are warm-blooded, have feathers and wings, and are two-legged

Fish—a group of animals that have a backbone, are cold-blooded, usually have scales and fins, live in water, and breathe with gills

Insects—a group of animals that do not have a backbone, and in the adult state have three main body parts and six legs

Tips

* Look around! Science is simply the study of the world around us.

* Take advantage of your child's natural interests, such as collecting bugs or digging holes.

* Turn your own hobbies, such as birdwatching or gardening, into science field trips or studies.

* Ordinary activities such as washing dishes, taking a bath, boiling water, or observing a thunderstorm can illustrate scientific concepts.

* Make sure you don't overwhelm your first-grade child with more information than he or she is ready to handle!

* When your child asks you questions, you may have to make a date to research the topic at a later time. Keep a list of possible investigations and field trips.

WATER

Investigations

Here are some questions to get you started on a study of water. Design a simple experiment or field trip to explore each topic.

* What objects will float in water? Which ones will sink?

* Can you float in the water in a pool? Can you float in the ocean? In which water is it easier to float? Why?

* What happens when you mix water with other substances?

* What substances dissolve in water? Which substances will not dissolve in water?

* What happens when you leave a shallow bowl of water on a sunny window ledge for a week?

* What causes water to turn into ice or steam, or back to water?

* What are fog, clouds, hail, rain, frost, or snow made of? How can you tell?

* Why does "steam" come out of our mouths when we speak and laugh outdoors on a frosty morning?

* Why do streams sometimes dry up?

* What causes flooding?

* How many inches of rain falls on your neighborhood during a rainstorm? How could you find out?

* How does water affect the growth of plants? How can you test your hypothesis?

* Where does your home water supply come from?

* Where does the water go after it goes down the drain?

Field Trips

At home or on vacation, you are sure to find water in some form.

* Hike along a stream, river, or lake.

* Explore life in a pond.

* Compare rocks you find in a river or by the sea to those you find on a dry mountain.

* Ride on a boat, raft, canoe, or inner tube.

* Swim in the ocean.

* Play in the snow—find a snowflake.

* View a museum exhibit on weather, the public water supply, or marine life.

* Visit a weather station.

* Visit a hydroelectric power plant or dam.

* Perform a taste test comparing the water in different towns and in different kinds of bottled water.

Helpful Equipment:

* small objects of assorted shapes and materials (some of which float)

* tea kettle or pan

* liquid measuring cup

* cooking thermometer

* freezer

* food coloring

* clean jars to collect samples

* radish or bean seeds

* library books on water and weather

* black cloth (to reveal a snowflake)

* magnifying glass or microscope

AIR

Investigations

Air is all around us. Here are some activities that will help you study the properties of air.

* Fill a balloon with air. Tie it closed. Try to hold it under water in the bathtub. Let it go. What happens? Why?

* Blow up a balloon. Hold it closed, but do not tie it. Hold the balloon under water and release it.

* Fill a balloon with air and let it go in the air. What happens? Why?

* Now blow up a balloon, but do not tie it. Then stretch the opening so that it makes a squealing sound. What makes the noise?

* Put a straw under water and blow.

* Fly a kite. Try it on a windy day and when the air is still. What makes it fly?

* Blow a whistle and guess what makes the noise.

* Watch the airplanes take off at an airport. Make paper airplanes and fly them.

* Study the wind. Watching a flag or windsock can help you see which way the wind blows. Can you think of another method?

* Have an adult help you see if you can sit on the bottom of the pool in water that is not too deep. Now try again wearing an inflated lifejacket. Is there a difference?

* Have an adult place a small candle in the bottom of a wide jar. After the adult lights the candle, put the lid on the jar. Observe. Does the candle continue to burn, go out immediately, or go out after a slight delay? Guess why.

* Go sailing or windsurfing. Or make a tiny sailboat and sail it in a pond.

Whirlybird

You can make a paper helicopter that flies through the air.

First, cut a rectangle of paper 2" x 8". Make a cut from the middle of one short edge down about three inches. Next, make two half-inch-long cuts on each long side about 3½ inches up from the other end.

Then fold the paper as shown below. Drop your helicopter from a high place. If it flips upside down, you will need to stick a paperclip on the bottom part to give that end more weight.

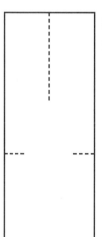

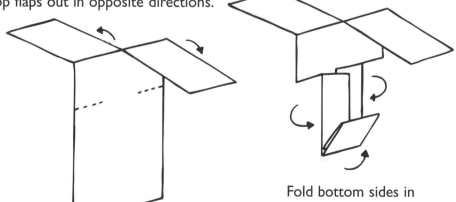

Fold top flaps out in opposite directions.

Fold bottom sides in and bend the tip up.

PLANTS

Looking at Plants

Here are some activities to begin your child's study of plants.

❋ Go on a leaf walk. Collect leaves of different shapes and colors, or draw pictures of the leaves you see. Look up the word leaf in the dictionary and in the encyclopedia. Can you find a chart showing different leaf shapes? You may need to visit the library. How many of the shapes did you find?

❋ The fruits and vegetables we eat come from plants. Collect seeds from fruits and vegetables your family eats. Ask a friend or relative to save seeds for you, too. Glue one of each kind of seed on separate cards and label them.

❋ Let some of the seeds you collected dry for a few days. Then plant them with moist soil in small paper cups near a sunny window. Poke a little hole in the bottom of each cup to let extra water drain out. Set the cups in a pan to catch the drips. Some seeds sprout quickly, some take a very long time.

❋ What kinds of seeds do people eat? Do you eat corn, popcorn, peas, beans, sunflower seeds, sesame seeds, or poppy seeds? Look for different kinds of seeds when you visit the grocery store.

❋ When the weather warms up in the spring, plant flowers or vegetables from seed. If you don't have a yard, grow them in a box or pot. Radishes and beets are easy to grow. Nasturtium flower seeds also grow well. What will your little plants need to grow well besides soil? Keep a journal describing the care you give your plants and how they grow.

❋ Trees are also plants. How many different kinds of trees can you find?

Taking a Closer Look

You will need clear plastic cups, paper towels, water, and seeds that are fairly large and easy to sprout, such as beans.

1. Line the sides of a cup with a paper towel. Put some crumpled paper towel in the middle to fill the cup halfway.

2. Slip some seeds between the paper towel and the cup, about halfway up the cup.

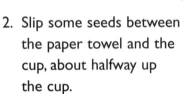

3. Add more crumpled paper towel in the middle to fill the cup. Make sure you can still see the seeds through the plastic. Moisten the paper towels.

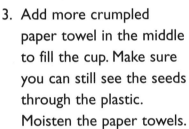

4. Place the cup in a warm, sunny place. Keep the paper towels moist. Watch what happens. Keep a journal of the changes you see.

5. Plant more seeds in the same way, but with these changes:

❋ leave some of the seeds dry

❋ grow some of the seeds in a dark place

❋ grow some of the seeds in a cold place

❋ grow some seeds covered by a glass jar
Compare your results.

Learning About Social Studies

First-grade social studies focus on life in the family and community. Topics might include community helpers; family customs; the need for rules in society; and how communities, families, and customs vary from culture to culture. In addition, the students will be introduced to patriotic symbols, such as the flag and the national anthem; to basic mapping skills; to the names of their city, state, and country; and to basic rights and responsibilities in a democracy, such as voting. They will probably discuss the election process and possibly vote on classroom decisions. First-grade students will be interested in learning to recognize the names and faces of important elected officials, such as the mayor or president. However, it will be several years before they have a clear understanding of government.

If you haven't already done so, now is a good time to hang a bulletin board for your child to post interesting news clippings, maps, photographs, family rules and jobs, and creative projects. A map of the country and a globe or world map will be helpful as you discuss world events and family travels.

Many children have no idea of the origin of their national flag. Colorful charts of the flags of the world can be found in most encyclopedias, atlases, and many dictionaries. Your child will enjoy looking through the many colorful national symbols. Then have your child draw and color a picture of a country's flag.

Your child may find a discussion of the rights and responsibilities of a citizen in a democracy a bit abstract. However, that same child will have very strong opinions on what is and is not fair in the family, in the neighborhood, and on the playground. Use these everyday situations to introduce concepts such as justice, democracy, and human rights and responsibilities.

SOCIAL STUDIES

Terms

Multicultural Awareness—recognizing and respecting differences and similarities between one's own culture and the many other cultures that make up a local or global community

Continents—the Earth's seven large bodies of land: North America, South America, Europe, Asia, Africa, Australia, and Antarctica (The Arctic area is not a land mass; it is ice floating on water.)

Oceans—the four main parts of the large body of salt water that covers about three-fourths of the Earth: Pacific Ocean, Atlantic Ocean, Indian Ocean, and Arctic Ocean

Compass Rose—the part of a map that shows directions (north, south, east, and west)

Legend or Key—the part of a map that explains symbols (pictures) used

Scale—the part of a map that shows how a distance on the map relates to the distance in the actual area shown; for example, one inch on the map represents one mile of actual distance

Pledge of Allegiance—

> I pledge allegiance to the flag of the United States of America and to the Republic for which it stands, one Nation under God, indivisible, with liberty and justice for all.

National Anthem—Each country has a special national song. In the United States, it is *The Star-Spangled Banner*:

> Oh! say, can you see, by the dawn's early light,
> What so proudly we hailed at the twilight's last gleaming?
> Whose broad stripes and bright stars, through the perilous fight,
> O'er the ramparts we watched were so gallantly streaming?
> And the rockets' red glare, the bombs bursting in air,
> Gave proof through the night that our flag was still there.
> Oh! say, does that star-spangled banner yet wave
> O'er the land of the free and the home of the brave?

Tips

✳ Avoid long, boring lectures. Adjust topics to your child's interest level.

✳ Find out the particular topics your child will study in class. Look for picture books at the library to supplement them.

✳ Collect pictures, brochures, and photographs to illustrate the information you study together.

✳ Realize that it may take many repetitions before your child remembers new information.

✳ Point out examples of "good citizenship" when you see them, such as a group cleaning up litter at the park.

✳ Introduce world geography whenever the opportunity arises. For example, find China on a globe after watching pandas at the zoo.

✳ If you have a computer system, your child may enjoy these CD-ROMs: *Trudy's Time and Place House* (Edmark) and *Where in the World Is Carmen Sandiego? Jr. Detective Edition* (Brøderbund).

OUR COMMUNITY

Who are the people in your family, neighborhood, school, and community? Your child can learn about the different roles individuals play in society at work, as volunteers, and in the home.

Families

* The next time you have a family gathering or look through your photo album, discuss relationships such as son, daughter, grandparent, aunt, uncle, and cousin. Your child can draw a picture of members of your family and label the relationships.

* Let your child interview adult relatives to find out about their occupations and volunteer work in the community. Collect the information in a home-made book. You might want to add snapshots as illustrations.

* Have your child draw a picture or write a description of your family's holiday customs, recipes, or country of origin.

* Help your child locate on a map or globe places where family members live or work.

Community Helpers

* Arrange to interview community workers such as the mail carrier, truck driver, doctor, city maintenance worker, or librarian. Find out how they help the community.

* Find out about volunteer opportunities in your community. (Your local newspaper office or the public library should have information.) Involve your child in a service project, such as recycling, collecting food for the needy, cleaning up a beach, or donating toys to a child-care center.

Field Trips

* Call and schedule visits to the police department, fire station, post office, city hall, or other public buildings and businesses.

* Take your child to visit the polling place on election day.

* Attend a patriotic celebration on Independence Day or on another national holiday.

Role-Playing

* Have a mock trial to decide a minor family dispute. Take turns being the judge, plaintiff, defendant, or member of the jury.

* Hold an election to make a family decision, such as where to go on a weekend outing. Count the ballots and announce the results.

* Play *What's My Line?*: Write community jobs on slips of paper. One player draws a job. The others ask questions that can be answered *yes* or *no* to discover the job.

Learning About Art

Children improve their dexterity as they work on the motivating art projects suggested in this section. Creating with paints, colored pens, folded paper, or modeling dough is great fun.

All school subjects overlap and art is no exception. You can use art projects to illustrate the writing activities or science explorations suggested in this book. You will also want your child to recognize the color words: *red, yellow, blue, green, orange, purple* (or *violet*), *pink, black, brown*, and *white*. The color words come up often in first-grade reading and activity books. Write these words on index cards and add them to your child's stack of reading flashcards.

Sets of nontoxic, felt-tip pens make a nice birthday or holiday gift. Felt pens are often easier to control than paints, and they produce richer, brighter colors than crayons. They come with fine points for drawing details and broad points for filling in large areas. Train your child to snugly replace the cap on each pen after it is used so the pens won't dry up.

You and your child can make greeting cards for all occasions. Have a paper cake pop out of a birthday card, a spider pop out of a scary card, or a heart pop out of a loving message. Use your imagination!

Art projects can make quite a mess. You might want to work outdoors or set up a table in the garage for painting activities. Expect that there will be drips and spills from time to time. Wear old clothes and keep paper towels and a damp sponge handy.

Professional artists don't always sit down and create a masterpiece on the first try. They often start over dozens of times before they are satisfied with their creations. So have extra materials on hand in case your little artist wants to make a fresh start.

Your child will be pleased if you find space to display the artwork. If possible, hang a bulletin board large enough to hold a calendar, a map, and your child's special creations. Your child will enjoy rearranging this display from time to time, adding snapshots, autumn leaves, award certificates, and other personal momentos.

ART—TERMS AND TIPS

Terms

Horizontal line—a line going across the page parallel to the bottom of the paper

Vertical line—a line going up and down on the page parallel to the side edge of the paper

Primary colors—red, yellow, blue

Secondary colors—orange, green, and purple made by mixing two primary colors

Warm colors—reds, oranges, yellows

Cool colors—blues, greens, purples

Collage—artwork made by pasting together bits and pieces on a surface

Tips

* Young children enjoy pounding, rolling, and creating with dough and clay even if they don't produce a recognizable product. They are learning about textures and shapes. Let them experiment.

* It is difficult for most young children to write and draw in a small space. Provide large paper for your child's writing and art projects.

* Ed Emberley writes how-to-draw books that most children enjoy. Look for *Ed Emberley's Drawing Book of Animals* and *Ed Emberley's Drawing Book: Make a World.*

* Use play dough to make animal figures and holiday decorations.

* Take your child on a visit to an art museum or look for library books with large color pictures of fine art. Your child may enjoy selecting a favorite artist. Many children are inspired by the bright colors and patterns of modern art paintings.

* Play the board game *Pictionary Junior* together to practice both reading and drawing.

* Look at Eric Carle's picture books such as *The Very Hungry Caterpillar* for a vibrant example of collage artwork. Your child can recycle old paintings, fingerpaintings, magazine pictures, and scraps of colored paper by cutting them up to use in a collage. Some artists add feathers, leaves, buttons, and other objects they find.

* Use inexpensive picture frames from the drugstore to display your child's artwork. Even random splashes of paint and colorful scribbles take on a new look in an attractive frame.

Learning About Music

First-grade children are just beginning to study music notation. They can clap to the beat of recorded music and accompany songs with homemade rhythm instruments. Reading the words to favorite songs is a motivating way to sneak in extra reading practice. And shy children learn to use their voices more forcefully as they belt out rousing melodies.

Raffi is one of the most popular artists performing for young children. Listen to a recording of his *Singable Songs for the Very Young*. If you and your child enjoy Raffi's music, you will want the *Raffi Singable Songbook* (Crown, 1980), which includes the words, music, and guitar chords for three of Raffi's popular recordings. Two great collections of traditional songs are *Tom Glazer's Treasury of Songs for Children* by Tom Glazer (Doubleday, 1988) and *Gonna Sing My Head Off!* by Kathleen Krull (Knopf, 1992).

Singing together can be great fun for the whole family. Play recordings of favorite tunes in the car on your next family trip and sing the miles away. Do you have a favorite song from your childhood? A holiday tune? A silly camp song? A patriotic song? A hymn? Teach it to your child! It will bring back warm memories.

At home, turn off the television and turn on the stereo or tape player. Background music can soothe nerves while lively music can wake up sleepyheads. Songs or instrumental pieces can inspire creative dramatics or brighten up a rainy day.

Your child will enjoy seeing musicians perform with real instruments. Get front row seats for performances by your high school band or orchestra. If you recognize some of the young people from your neighborhood, ask them to give your child a personal demonstration of their instruments. Your city's department of recreation, the school district, or a local college may provide free or inexpensive concerts especially for young children. A free concert in the park may be more appropriate for a wiggly child than a formal concert-hall performance. Your child may want to get up and dance!

MUSIC

Rhythm—the time, tempo, or meter of the music; the pattern of accented and unaccented beats

Pitch—the high or low tone of a musical note

Melody—the notes that make up the tune

Musical Notes—marks indicating the pitch and duration of the tone to be played

Rests—marks used to indicate a pause in the music

Staff—five parallel lines on which the musical notes are drawn (notes drawn higher on the staff are higher in pitch than those drawn lower on the staff)

whole note   half note   quarter note   eighth note   whole rest   half rest   quarter rest   eighth rest

Tips

* Turn the radio dial and expose your children to different types of music—classical, jazz, country, rock, rap. Talk about the differences you hear.

* Many libraries offer cassettes and CDs for checkout. This is a free way to explore different styles, composers, or performers.

* Listen to different instrumental pieces and have your child move to the music. What determines the mood of a piece? the instruments? the volume? the tempo (speed)?

* Listen to a recording of "Peter and the Wolf." This piece by Prokofiev introduces children to instruments in the symphony as it tells the story of Peter's adventures catching a wolf.

* The next time you rent a video, look for sing-along ones. The lyrics are shown on the screen so children can follow the bouncing ball to sing along.

* Listen to the soundtracks of musicals or watch the movie versions. Chores may be more fun to do on Saturday morning if you are singing along to *The Sound of Music, Camelot, West Side Story*, or *The Phantom of the Opera*.

* If you have a computer system, your child may enjoy these CD-ROMs: *Lamb Chop Loves Music* (Phillips) [designed for young children] and *Musical Instruments* (Microsoft) [designed for all ages].

Learning About Physical Education

Many parents do not realize the importance of physical education. Active games relieve stress, promote physical fitness, and build friendships. The process of organizing games teaches cooperation, leadership, and a respect for rules. Many childhood games also reinforce counting and alphabet skills. As children improve their coordination and playing skills, their self-esteem improves, and they gain the respect of their classmates. And children find it easier to sit still and focus on academic tasks after they run off some of their excess energy. So physical education plays an important part in every well-balanced educational program.

Young children are not usually ready for highly competitive sports. They need to develop throwing, catching, kicking, running, and jumping skills first in less stressful situations. Playing catch is a great way to work on throwing and catching skills with your child, but don't start out with a hard baseball. Children become afraid of the ball once a hard ball hits them. Really timid children can start out tossing and catching a pillow. Then tennis balls can be used for catching and batting practice instead of baseballs.

Common children's games are played in many variations all over the world. This book provides you with popular versions, but you may want to

consult with older children in your school or neighborhood to learn the rules played in your area.

DETERMINING WHO IS "IT"

Some games require one player to be "It." There are many ways to decide who will be "It" first. Here is one way:

When a group of players decides on a game, any quick-thinking player cries out, "Not It!" and extends one hand. The other players cry out, "Not It!" and add a hand to the pile. The last player to call out is "It."

TAG

Define the boundaries of the play area and decide who is "It." This player chases the other players. The first player tagged is now "It" and must try to tag the other players. No fair tagging the player who just tagged you!

Freeze Tag Variation—Start out the same as basic tag. However, a tagged player must freeze. "It" tries to freeze all of the players. If another player who is still free tags a frozen player, the frozen player is free to run again.

Group Tag Variation—Start out the same as basic tag. However, a tagged player joins "It" and helps catch the other players. Eventually, all the players will be helping "It" catch the last runner. The last player captured becomes "It" for the next game.

Hug Tag Variation—Start out the same as basic tag. However, a player can't be tagged if he or she is hugging another player. The time limit for a hug is five seconds. So players hug and run to find another safe player.

Social Skills

Your child's school experiences will be much more enjoyable if you have taken the time to work on social skills at home. This section covers topics such as getting along with others, making friends, using good manners, following school rules, and knowing what to do in an emergency.

Good communication skills are essential for getting along in the classroom and on the playground. Review page 18 in the Language Arts section for activities that will develop your child's speaking ability.

ROLE-PLAYING ACTIVITIES

If you do a little role-playing in advance, your child will be better prepared to handle unusual situations. Here are some that may arise:

* Another child takes your child's lunch or jacket by accident

* An older child bothers your child on the playground

* A strange adult offers your child a ride

* Your child forgets his or her lunch money

* Your child does not understand the instructions on a classroom assignment

* Your child wishes to join a game at recess

* Your child needs to use the bathroom during class (or, oops, has an accident)

* Your child feels sick during school

* Someone calls your child a rude name

* Your child's nose begins to run in school

You don't want to overwhelm your child with too many scary possibilities! Just for fun, try playing the part of the child yourself, and let your child be the teacher or scary stranger. A little humor will make this necessary discussion less frightening.

SEPARATION ANXIETY

Some children become anxious when they leave home to go to school. Here are some tips to help your child bear the separation.

* Plan with your child what to do if the carpool or bus is not there at the regular time.

* If possible, tour the campus before school begins, locating the office, restrooms, cafeteria, playground, and your child's assigned classroom.

* Write little love messages to tuck in the lunch box.

* Tape a photo of your family in the lunch box lid.

* Talk to your child if school has become a worry. Sometimes there is a specific problem you can correct.

For example, your child may not know how to use the toilet in the public rest rooms. Or there may be a bully on the school bus upsetting your child.

SELF-ESTEEM

Children need to know that their parents love and accept them. Enjoy your own special child whether tall or short, chubby or thin, shy or outgoing, fearless or timid. Don't get caught up in comparing your child to other children. Nobody is perfect. We all have different strengths and weaknesses, quirks and enthusiasms. Love yourself and your child—you are delightful, interesting, imperfect human beings!

PROMOTING INDEPENDENCE

If you arrange your home to be "child friendly," your child will be able to take care of most of his or her own needs independently. Obviously, first-grade children should not be left alone. But neither should they be dependent on constant adult attention. Here are some suggestions to develop independence.

✳ Select comfortable clothing that is easy to get on and off.

✳ Put up low shelves and hooks to store your child's belongings within reach.

✳ Provide a stepstool that won't tip over.

✳ Involve your child in simple cooking and housekeeping duties, such as making sandwiches or wiping the kitchen table.

Communication

One of the best ways you can encourage your child's self-confidence is to listen attentively. Your child will enjoy discussing where to go on a family outing, the pros and cons of hamsters as pets, or what to serve for dinner next week. Ask for your child's advice when you select gifts for your nieces and nephews. Allow your child to make choices whenever possible. Let him or her make clothing decisions, select the gift to take to a party, or order a meal from a restaurant menu.

STRENGTHS AND WEAKNESSES

Most people have a bad day every now and then where they feel they are just not good at anything. If it happens to your child, you may want to share a similar day you had as a child. Then have your child make two lists—one titled *Things I am pretty good at* and the other *Things I wish I were* *better at*. (You may want to do this activity simultaneously to help your child recognize that adults aren't good at everything either.) Compare your child's list of his or her own strengths to those you see in your child. (They may be quite different and enlightening to both of you!) Then go through the list of things your child would like to be better at. Let your child choose one that is important to him or her and challenge your child to think of ways of improving. Support your child's efforts when possible and gently guide your child when needed.

MAKING FRIENDS

Remember how important it was for you to have friends when you were a child? It is not necessary for your child to win a popularity contest, but every child needs one or two good buddies to play with at recess or to call to find out about a confusing homework assignment or holiday schedule. Here are ideas for helping your child make friends.

✳ Attend parent orientation meetings at the school and invite several other parents and children to get together for a play date at the park or in your home.

✳ Encourage your child to invite different classmates home to play (one at a time). Sometimes a friendship may spark when away from the group pressures at school.

✳ If your child is shy and wants playmates but doesn't have any, speak with your child's teacher. He or she may be able to suggest children that you don't know who might get along well with your child.

✳ Although it is not good to over-schedule your child, do sign up for at least one extra-curricular activity if possible. Participating in sports, scouting, or religious activities are all great ways to find friends.

✳ Make friends with the parents of children your child's age. Consider baby-sitting for one another from time to time.

✳ Go to the playground on weekends and help your child practice the games that are popular at recess.

PLAYING WITH FRIENDS

✳ Once your child finds a friend, include that friend in some of your family activities, such as a Friday night dinner or swimming at the community pool.

✳ Encourage your child to exchange phone numbers with special friends. Write them in your family directory.

✳ Be nearby, but don't intervene in conflicts unless someone is in physical danger. Learning how to work through disagreements is an important part of being a friend.

✳ Allow your child to invite special friends to a simple holiday party. Young children are generally happier if there are not too many guests.

RULES AND PROCEDURES

Part of living in a community is respecting the rules that help it prosper. It is important for your child to recognize that different places have different rules. What is OK at your friend's home may not be OK at your home. What the music teacher allows may not be what the regular classroom teacher requires. Teach your child to respect the rules of the person in charge. If a classroom or school rule strongly conflicts with your personal beliefs, speak to the teacher privately. Most times an alternative can be agreed to that supports the overall objective yet honors the needs of all involved.

School Rules

Ask in the office for a printed copy of your school's rules to discuss with your child. Rules vary by school, but here are some common ones:

✳ Students will treat each other with respect.

✳ Students must take care of school property.

✳ Running is allowed only on the playground.

✳ Students should arrive at school well before the tardy bell, but not before the staff is on duty. (Ask in the office if you do not know what time the campus opens.)

✳ All adults visiting the school must check in through the office.

✳ Children require a note to return to school after an absence.

Classroom Rules

You may receive information about the rules and procedures in your child's specific class. Here are some common classroom rules and procedures:

✳ Raise your hand when you wish to contribute to a class discussion.

✳ Be kind with your words and actions.

✳ Work without disturbing others.

✳ Keep your hands to yourself.

✳ Clean up any mess you make.

✳ Ask permission before leaving to use the restroom.

✳ Bring toys and other personal objects to school only when needed for Show-and-Tell or other scheduled activities.

SPECIAL PROCEDURES

✳ Find out how the school deals with children who forget or lose their lunch or lunch money.

✳ Locate the safest place to drop off and pick up your child before and after school.

✳ Find out how your school will notify parents if school is canceled due to snow or other emergencies.

✳ Discuss with your child what to do if he or she misses the bus, the carpool fails to arrive, or it starts to rain.

Home and School Cooperation

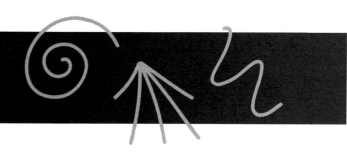

Plan to attend parent orientation meetings at your child's school to find out about school rules and procedures. If that is not possible, ask in the office for a printed copy of orientation materials. Your child will feel more secure if you are knowledgeable about school holidays, lunch money, bus schedules, dress codes, and daily routines. If you have questions, the school secretary can be an invaluable resource. But please note, the 15 minutes in the morning just before school starts can be very busy in a school office! Try to arrive early, or visit at another time of day so that the staff members can give you their full attention.

Most schools have a Back-to-School Night or Open House when parents can visit the classroom in the evening. Remember that the teacher cannot discuss individual students at this time. Save specific questions and concerns about your child for a private parent-teacher conference.

Be sure to set a good example for your child by treating school staff members with respect and courtesy. Children can feel lost and lonely at school surrounded by unfamiliar faces. Take the time to introduce your child to the school secretary, nurse, crossing guard, bus driver, principal, custodian, and playground supervisors, as well as to the classroom teacher and teaching assistant. You can even take snapshots of staff members and post them, with their names and titles, on your family bulletin board or refrigerator. Problems at school are much more manageable if your child knows a friendly adult to turn to for help.

Some schools try to schedule a conference with each child's parent during a particular week of the school year. However, you can call the school office to arrange a meeting anytime you think it is necessary. Jot down the topics you would like to discuss as they occur to you so that you will be ready for your conference. Bring your written questions and concerns along on the day of the conference. Remember that human beings, including teachers, don't like to be attacked. Assume that the teacher is your friend and partner working with you to help your child, and word your concerns accordingly.

GETTING ORGANIZED

Good routines will help your child arrive at school safe, well-rested, on time, and ready to work.

BEDTIMES

Make sure your child gets enough rest. Remember, children need more sleep than adults! Academic work suffers when children are tired and cranky. Set a regular bedtime, and stick to it except for very special occasions. A bedtime ritual with a story, comforting nightlight, and three big hugs will help your child accept this important rule.

MORNING MADNESS

Sometimes it seems impossible to get a family fed, dressed, and ready for work and school on time. Here are some suggestions to make the morning hours go more smoothly:

* Set out clothing and shoes the night before.

* Pack lunches or hand out lunch money the night before.

* When you cash a paycheck, get some change and small bills.

* Always place backpacks and keys in the same place, and have an extra set of keys as back up.

* Pack homework and signed notes in the child's folder or backpack as soon as completed—the night before!

* Make sure everyone has a spare pair of shoes in case one shoe is wet or missing.

* If you seem to be running late most days, set bedtimes and wake-up times back a half hour. Rushing every day can be stressful.

* Take time to eat breakfast. If you and your child dislike traditional breakfast foods, eat a sandwich, milkshake, yogurt, leftovers, or any other healthful food you enjoy.

TRANSPORTATION

Whether your child rides the bus, walks to school, joins a carpool, or rides in your car to school, safety is important!

* Introduce your child to the crossing guard.

* Point out crosswalks and traffic signals.

* Practice walking to and from the school or bus stop with your child.

* Use your judgment—not all first graders are ready to walk to school independently.

* Make friends with your neighbors so that they can provide assistance in an emergency. Make sure your child knows which neighbors to contact for help.

* Ask an older child who rides the school bus to look out for your child on the bus.

HOMEWORK

The amount and type of homework assigned in a first-grade classroom will vary. Some teachers do not assign any homework. Others assign detailed work that takes up to an hour to complete (including unfinished work from the school day). Homework may include activities such as these: read aloud 15 minutes, review flashcards, practice spelling words, make up characters for a story, collect leaves for science, get your permission slip signed.

Your child will need a work space to do homework. It may be a desk in his or her room. Or it may be the kitchen table. Gather and store needed supplies in a box. The key is to have the supplies ready so your child can focus on the work.

HOMEWORK TIPS

✳ Decide with your child the best time to work on homework each day and designate it as "homework hour."

✳ Stick to the regularly scheduled homework time except for very special occasions.

✳ Turn off the TV and limit distractions.

✳ Have your own activity to do, such as chopping vegetables or folding laundry, so you can stay nearby without becoming overly involved in your child's homework.

✳ Have your child pack the homework in a folder or backpack as soon as it is finished.

✳ Realize your child is 6 or 7 years old and don't expect perfection.

✳ Ask your child's teacher for suggestions. If the amount or level of homework is overwhelming, most teachers will adjust it.

If you think your child does not have enough homework, don't panic. Your child works hard at school. He or she needs time to relax and play. Remember— you and your child can read aloud, cook, play games, plant a garden, go bike riding, and enjoy all the activities described in this book. Even without written drillwork, your child will be learning and growing each day!

Work Space Supplies

✳ pencils (soft lead—#2)

✳ erasers (Make sure they really erase!)

✳ pencil sharpener

✳ ruler (with centimeters and inches)

✳ crayons

✳ colorful, nontoxic felt pens

✳ scissors (Make sure they really cut!)

✳ glue sticks, paste, or nontoxic glue

✳ stapler

✳ old magazines (to cut out pictures)

✳ lined paper (for writing activities)

✳ blank paper (for drawing)

✳ dictionary

RESOURCES AND PROGRAMS

There are many school, district, county, state, and federal programs set up to help children and families. Your child may be eligible for one of these programs:

* tutoring

* speech therapy

* classes for the gifted

* classes for the hearing- or sight-impaired

* physical therapy

* workshops for dealing with divorce or death

* summer school classes

* free or subsidized breakfast or lunch

* subsidized after-school care

If your child has special needs, arrange a conference with the teacher and principal. They may also request a school counselor or psychologist to attend as well. If your neighborhood school does not have the necessary resources to meet your child's needs, free bus transportation is often provided to another school site in the area.

The staff at your child's school will try to meet every child's needs, but they may be overworked and underfunded. It might take them too long to arrange for the special services for your child. Don't wait, investigate! It is never too soon—infant and preschool programs are often available for children with special needs. Consider joining a parent support group for families with similar interests. Experienced parents can tell you about their experiences, community resources, and the best programs available. You can begin the search for interest groups and support services in your area by asking the reference librarian at the

Tip! If you find professionals using terms you are not familiar with, such as IEP (Individual Education Plan), tell them to pause and define the terms.

public library or by looking in the Government or Community Services pages in your telephone directory. It will probably take several phone calls to track down the services and organizations you need. There are also many resources and parent groups available through the Internet.

Be aware that names of educational programs and services may vary from school to school and district to district. For example, programs for the gifted might be called G.A.T.E. (Gifted and Talented Education), M.G.M. (Mentally Gifted Minors), T.A.G. (Talented and Gifted), A.L.P. (Accelerated Learning Program), or any other clever acronym the administrators come up with!

Pencil Toppers and Bookmarks

Berry Good!

Purr-fect!

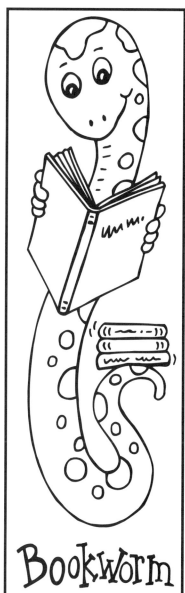

Bookworm

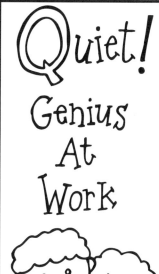

Quiet! Genius At Work

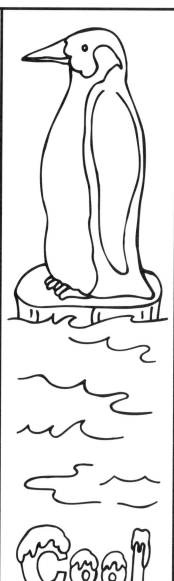

Cool

Backs of Rewards